THE STAGES OF
HIGHER KNOWLEDGE

By

RUDOLF STEINER

Anthroposophic Press

The German original of this book bears the title, *Die Stufen der hoeheren Erkenntnis* (No. 12 in the *Bibliographical Survey*, 1961). It was formerly published in English under the title, *The Gates of Knowledge*. Revised translation by Lisa D. Monges and Floyd McKnight.

Library of Congress Catalog Card No. 67-24379

This translation has been authorized for the Western Hemisphere by agreement with the Rudolf Steiner Nachlassverwaltung, Dornach, Switzerland.

PRINTED IN THE UNITED STATES OF AMERICA

CONTENTS

TRANSLATOR'S NOTE

FEELING A MORAL RESPONSIBILITY to convey, as far as is possible in any translation, the original meaning intended by the author, the translator has used the word "representation" wherever "Vorstellung" appeared. Thus it is distinguished from "Idee" even though both these different words are frequently rendered as "idea" in English. As Dr. H. Poppelbaum noted in his preface to the revised 1939 translation of *The Philosophy of Spiritual Activity,* the word "representation," however clumsy it may seem at first glance, "is justified, because the mental picture indeed stands for the concept and *represents* it." The difficulty in translating the word "Vorstellung," however, is acknowledged and further emphasized by a more recent translator, Michael Wilson. He, in his Introduction to his translation of the same work re-titled, *The Philosophy of Freedom* (1966), explains his use of the term "mental image" as being more accurate for English usage. Interested readers are referred to these two translators for a full exposition of the problem.

Rudolf Steiner's original paragraphing, undoubtedly regarded at first as a stumbling block by some readers, also has been retained in this translation. This is because, carefully and deliberately arrived at by the author, it is an essential part of the whole work, helping to express what was meant.

PREFACE
by Marie Steiner

THE MAGAZINE, *Lucifer,* edited by Rudolf Steiner in the service of spiritual science, was enlarged in 1904 through the merger with the Austrian magazine, *Gnosis.* Thenceforth it bore the double name, *Lucifer-Gnosis.* In it were published Rudolf Steiner's articles that later appeared as the book, *Knowledge of the Higher Worlds and Its Attainment,* which, with the books, *Theosophy* and *Occult Science, an Outline,* belongs to the basic works of the anthroposophically oriented science of the spirit.

A continuation of these articles appeared under the title, *The Stages of Higher Knowledge.* They were intended, later on, to be formed into a second volume in continuation of *Knowledge of the Higher Worlds and Its Attainment.* But an overabundance of work and the heavy demands that lecturing made upon his time gradually prevented Rudolf Steiner from devoting the necessary attention to the magazine, although there was a steady increase in the number of its readers. As a result, its publication had to cease, and the further appearance of the articles on *The Stages of Higher Knowledge* had to be interrupted.

We have often been asked to make them available again through a new edition. The present books complies with this wish. Since the text suddenly breaks off, the book cannot claim the value of completeness. It was, therefore, justifiable to question the advisability of a new edition. The views presented here, but not brought to a conclusion, have been published many times in other written works of Rudolf Steiner in a different form and under different titles. But for the searcher of the spirit the fact remains that the conquest of spiritual reality is possible only by returning again and again to the spiritual contents once worked over but never sufficiently assimilated, and by experiencing ever anew the path that once has shown the direction into the realm of the spirit. The soul life of the person working meditatively must be kept so mobile that the view afforded him by one path makes him all the more receptive to views from other aspects.

The articles published here are of historical value. They indicate the starting-point of Rudolf Steiner's esoteric instructions; they show us how he has become the pioneer in this very domain in which, through his indications, man for the first time has been allowed freedom. With a world-encompassing outlook, and a high sense of responsibility he had to build a basis and create a spiritual attitude through which man — by finding within himself the solid moral support — might still in this freedom avoid falling prey to temptation and aberration. In order to accomplish such a deed at a decisive turning-point in history, in the midst of opposing forces, relying solely upon one's own self, there was needed the tremendous ethical power that permeates Rudolf Steiner's entire life-work, its goals the welfare of mankind, the rescue of the Western world from the threatening collapse. He laid the foundations for his work in a way that corresponded with the demands of the age. To achieve this required the synthesis of all knowledge.

If one takes up these articles, written at the beginning of an astonishing life work that continued until March

30, 1925, and that, in the first years of this century, had received an impulse willed by destiny through its connection with theosophical groups fed from oriental sources — the question arises: How is it to be understood that Rudolf Steiner, who pointed the way to freedom also in esoteric life, to full self-reliance, and who let the pupil pledge to his own higher ego the obedience he must otherwise pledge to the teacher — how is it to be understood that Rudolf Steiner still urges in these articles the necessity of a strict reliance of the student upon the teacher, making the student as it were dependent upon the teacher?

In truth, Rudolf Steiner is only describing the pupil-teacher relationship as one of trust. From the very beginning he has avoided and rejected the authoritative element. In ancient times, the initiating priests took full responsibility for initiation of the neophyte into the mysteries of spiritual existence and exerted their will upon him. Thus the pupil was at the same time protected and guided, and was able to escape the dangers that otherwise would have overpowered him. His ego still hovered above his physical sheaths; his consciousness of self had not yet awakened. To awaken it more and more was the task of the progressing mystery training.

By drawing attention to the Cosmic Teacher, Christian initiation lessened the dependency upon the personal teacher, without wholly eliminating it. In the Rosicrucian training this dependency gradually loses its personal character and transforms itself into a relationship of trust. The teacher assists the student, shows him the way he seeks but cannot find unaided. The teacher gives him moral support, points out the dangers of vanity and the trickery of deceptive images that he must learn to distinguish from true spiritual reality. Thus the teacher is a helper ready to withdraw when trust is lacking.

At the turning-point of history at which we stand, the teacher working for the present had to point to the past, present, and future of human spiritual striving and, beginning with the education of the individual, had to erect his work so that it constituted a deed for mankind: a newly-gained element of life for posterity. Thus, Rudolf Steiner created a science of initiation in which henceforth every serious, morally striving human being can find the fundament that carries him; he will be able to take hold of the elements that sharpen his power of discrimination while new worlds open up to him. He need not grope uncertainly, having received enough instruction to guide him until he finds the leader in the lands of spirit.

This was not the case before Rudolf Steiner began his spiritual work. His deed is the *science* of initiation. Through it is revealed what lay hidden in the Mysteries of the ancient temples: namely, alongside the knowledge of cosmic evolution, the knowledge of the imminent descent of Christ, and what was sealed up in the Church: the redeeming deed of the liberation of mankind through the Christ and the gradual permeation of the ego of the individual with His power. Instead of personal guidance, the requirement now is that the human being find the way to the Ego of Mankind, to the Christ, through the forces of the time spirit. The consciousness of the individual human being is made mature for the acceptance of the higher ego force; self-consciousness is raised to spirit self.

It is the work of the future. But only by standing on the ground of the past and preparing the future can man work fruitfully for the present. By any other course he strives in the void. Here, too, the laws of metamorphosis govern. The future is created through transformation of the present that is rooted in the past. New elements appear, just as the new spring follows the winter. The power of the sun glows through the earth; all that decays, undergoing transformation, is kindled to new life through grace descending from above.

Also in the esoteric realm happenings unfold in historical continuity, in accordance with the law of ascending evolution and the flood tide and ebb tide of diminishing and flourishing life until the seemingly sudden moment when the rays of grace break forth, like the miracle of the radiant blossom in the green plant world. Yet without this transformation from form to form carried out by wise powers, and the constant enhancement in all domains of life, the new values, the gifts of the spirit, the fiery tongues of the Word would not descend upon us. Without knowledge of such happenings, the recipients of these gifts would not be in a position to grasp what it is that wants to take place among them. The great new power could not become effective, the future could not be saved.

The souls striving for spiritual knowledge who approached Rudolf Steiner were the human material willed by destiny and led to him by the age with whom Rudolf Steiner had to work. Out of their needs and requirements he had to form the science of initiation, based on cognition. It was his task to tear men away from the indolence of the age in regard to the spirit, so that they could become a bridge for the demands of the future.

Most difficult was the awakening of a sense for inner freedom, self-reliance, fully answerable to itself. With scrupulous regard for this goal, Rudolf Steiner desired no other role among men than that of instructor and, when so requested, advisor, awakener to spiritual goals of mankind. He was able to present spiritual facts because his thinking and beholding were permeated with life and unfolded, step by step, with the power of an organism of nature. His spiritual work stands before us — the restored unity of science, art and religion.

From the Preface for the Edition of September, 1914, of Rudolf Steiner's Book, KNOWLEDGE OF THE HIGHER WORLDS AND ITS ATTAINMENT

W HEN I WROTE the essays that constitute this book, much had to be discussed in a different way from today, because at that time I had to allude in a different manner to the substance of what has since been published concerning facts of cognition of spiritual worlds. In my book, *An Outline of Occult Science,* in *The Spiritual Guidance of Mankind,* in *A Road to Self-Knowledge* and especially in *The Threshold of the Spiritual World,* as well as in other writings, spiritual processes are described whose existence, to be sure, was already indicated in this book ten years ago, but in words differing from those that seem right today. At that time I had to explain that a great deal of what was not yet described in the book could be learned by oral communication. Much of this material has since been published. But allusions to it before publication left the possibility of misinterpretation and misunderstanding on the part of the reader. It might be possible, for instance, to imagine something much more vital in the personal relations between the seeker for spiritual schooling and this or that teacher than is intended. I trust I have here succeeded, by presenting details in a certain way, in emphasizing more strongly that for one seeking spiritual schooling in accord with present spiritual conditions an absolute direct relation to the objective spiritual world is of far greater importance than a relation to the personality of a teacher. The latter will gradually become merely the helper; he will assume the same position in spiritual schooling as a teacher occupies, in conformity with modern views, in any other field of knowledge. I believe I have sufficiently stressed the fact that the teacher's authority and the pupil's faith in him should play no greater part in spiritual schooling than in any other branch of knowledge or life. A great deal depends, it seems to me, upon an increasingly true estimate of this relation between the one who carries on spiritual research and those who develop an interest in the results of his research. Thus I believe I have improved the book wherever I was in a position, after ten years, to find what needs improving.

A second part is to be added to this first part, bringing further explanations of the frame of mind that can lead a man to the experience of the higher worlds.

RUDOLF STEINER

Berlin, September 7, 1914

THE STAGES OF HIGHER KNOWLEDGE

IN MY BOOK, *Knowledge of the Higher Worlds and Its Attainment,* the path to higher knowledge has been traced up to the meeting with the two Guardians of the Threshold. The relation in which the soul stands to the different worlds as it passes through the successive stages of knowledge will now be described. What will be given may be called "the teachings of occult science."

Before man enters upon the path of higher knowledge, he knows only the first of four stages of cognition. This stage is the one he occupies in ordinary life in the world of the senses. Even in what is called science, we have to do only with this first stage of knowledge, for science merely elaborates ordinary cognition more minutely and in a disciplined way. Aided by instruments — the microscope, the telescope, and so forth — the senses examine their surroundings *with greater exactness* than they could without these aids. Yet man remains at the same stage of cognition whether he sees large things with the naked eye or observes small objects and phenomena with the aid of a microscope. Also in the application of thinking to facts and things, this science remains in the realm of everyday life. Man arranges the objects, describes and compares them, seeks to picture to himself their variations, and so forth. The keenest scientist does nothing fundamentally, in this respect, but develop to a fine art the methods of observing everyday life. His knowledge embraces a wider range, becomes more complex and more logical, but he does not proceed to any other *mode of cognition.*

In occult science this *first* stage of knowledge is called the "material mode of cognition." This is followed by *three* higher stages, and there are still others beyond these. These stages of knowledge shall be described here before

3

proceeding with the description of the "path of knowledge." Considering the ordinary method of scientific cognition, of apprehension through the senses as the first stage, we shall have to differentiate the following four stages:

1. Material knowledge.
2. Imaginative knowledge.
3. Inspirational knowledge, which may also be called "of the nature of will."
4. Intuitive knowledge.

These stages will be discussed here. It must first be made quite clear what is significant in these different modes of cognition. — In the ordinary sense knowledge four elements are to be considered: (1) *the object,* which makes an impression upon the senses; (2) *the image,* which the human being forms of this object; (3) *the concept,* through which the human being arrives at a spiritual comprehension of an object or an event; (4) *the ego,* which forms for itself the image and concept based on the impression of the object. Before the human being makes for himself an image, a 'representation," an object is there that causes it. He does not form the object, he perceives it, and on the basis of this object, the image arises. As long as we are looking at an object, we have to do with the thing itself. The moment we turn away from it, we have left only the *image.* The object is relinquished, the image is retained in the memory. But one cannot stop here at the image-making stage. One must go on to "concepts." The distinction between "image" and "concept" is absolutely necessary if we are to be clear at this point. Suppose one sees an object of circular form. Then one turns away and retains the *picture* of the circle in memory. So far one has not yet the "concept" of the circle. One attains this concept only when one says to oneself, "A circle is a figure in which all points are equidistant from the center." Understanding of a thing is attained only when a "concept" of it has been formed. There are all kinds of circles — small, large, red, blue, and so forth — but there is only one concept "circle." — All these things will be approached more closely; for the moment it will suffice to sketch what is necessary to characterize the first four stages of knowledge. — The fourth element that comes under consideration in material cognition is the "ego." In it the union of images and concepts is produced. The ego stores up the image in memory. Otherwise no continuing inner life would be possible. The images of things would remain only so long as the things themselves affected the soul. But the inner life depends upon the linking of one perception with another. The ego orients itself in the world today because in the presence of certain objects the images of similar objects of yesterday arise. It is obvious that soul life would be impossible if the image of a thing could be held only as long as the thing itself was present. — In relation to concepts also, the ego forms the unity. It combines its concepts and so makes a survey, calls forth an understanding of the world. This linking up of concepts is what occurs in "forming judgments." A being possessing only loosely connected concepts would not find his way in the world. All man's activity depends on his capacity to combine concepts — that is, to "form judgments."

The "material mode" of cognition rests upon the fact that man receives through his senses an impression of things and representations of the outer world. He has the power of sensing, or sensibility. The impression received from "outside" is also called *sensation*. Therefore in "material cognition" four elements have to be considered: Sensation, image, concept, ego. — At the next higher stage of knowledge, the impression made upon the outer senses, the "sensation," falls away. There is no longer any outer sensory object. Of the elements to which man is accustomed in ordinary knowledge there remains only the three: Image, concept and ego.

Ordinary knowledge in a healthy individual creates no image and no concept when an object does not confront the outer senses. The ego then remains inactive. Whoever forms images of which the corresponding sensory objects do not actually exist lives in fantasy. — But the occult student acquires this very faculty of forming images without the stimulus of external sensory objects. With him something else must take the place of outer objects. He must be able to form images although no object touches his senses. Something must step in to replace sensation. This something is *Imagination*. At this stage, images appear to the occult student in exactly the same way as if a sensory object were making an impression upon him. They are as vivid and true as sensory images, yet they are not of material, but of soul-spirit origin. Yet the senses remain entirely inactive. — It is evident that the individual must first acquire this faculty of forming *meaningful images* without sense impressions. This is accomplished through meditation and through the exercises that have been described in the book, *Knowledge of the Higher Worlds and Its Attainment*. The man confined to the sense world lives only among images that have reached him through the senses. The imaginative man has a world of images that he has received from a higher source. A careful training is necessary to distinguish illusion from reality in this higher image world. When such images first enter a man's soul he tends to say, "Ah! that is only fancy; a mere outflow of my life of thoughts." This is only too understandable, for man is at present accustomed to term "real" only what is given to him on the sure foundation of the evidence of his senses without effort on his part. He must first accustom himself to accept as "real" things that originate from a different side. In this respect he cannot guard too carefully against becoming a visionary. The capacity to decide what is "real" and what is "illusionary" in these higher regions can come only from experience, and this experience must be made one's own in a quiet, patient inner life. One must be fully prepared to expect the nasty tricks that illusion plays upon one. Everywhere lurks the possibility that images will emerge that result from delusions of the outer senses, or of abnormal life. All such possibility must first be done away with. One must first completely stop up the springs of the fantastic; only thus can one come to Imagination. At this point it will be clear that the world that one has entered in this way is not only just as real as the world of sense, *but much more real.*

In the *third* stage of knowledge, images no longer appear. The human being has now to deal only with "concept" and "ego." Whereas at the second stage a world of images still surrounded one, remainder of the moment when a vivid memory instantaneously kindles impressions from the outer world, without oneself actually having such impressions, at the third stage not even such images are present. The human being lives wholly in a purely spiritual world. One accustomed to hold strictly to

7

the senses will be tempted to believe this world pale and ghostly. But that is not at all the case. Neither has the world of images of the second stage anything pale or shadowy about it. So, to be sure, are the images that remain in memory after the outer objects are no longer there. But the pictures of Imagination have a vivacity and a comprehensiveness with which the shadowy memory pictures of the sensory world, and even the glittering and ephemeral physical world itself are not to be compared. This, too, is but a shadow compared to the realm of Imagination. — Now the world of the third stage of knowledge! Nothing in the sensory world can even suggest its wealth and abundance. What was sensation at the first stage of cognition, imagination at the second, here becomes "inspiration." Inspiration gives the impressions, and the ego forms the concepts. If anything at all in the realm of sense can be compared with this world of Inspiration, it is the world of tone opened up to us by the sense of hearing. But now not the tones of earthly music are concerned, but purely "spiritual tones." One begins to "hear" what is going on at the heart of things. The stone, the plant, and so forth, become "spiritual words." The world begins to express its true nature to the soul. It sounds grotesque, but it is literally true, that at this stage of knowledge one "hears spiritually the growing of the grass." The crystal form is perceived like sound; the opening blossom "speaks" to men. The inspired man is able to proclaim the inner nature of things; everything rises up before his soul, as though from the dead, in a new kind of way. He speaks a language that stems from another world, and that alone can make the everyday world comprehensible.

8

Lastly, at the *fourth* stage of knowledge Inspiration also ceases. Of the elements customarily observed in everyday knowledge, the ego alone remains to be considered. The attainment of this stage by the occult student is marked by a definite inner experience. This experience manifests itself in the feeling that he no longer stands outside the things and occurrences that he recognizes, but is himself within them. Images are not the object, but merely its imprint. Also, inspiration does not yield up the object itself, but only tells about it. But what now lives in the soul is in reality the object itself. The ego has streamed forth over all beings; it has merged with them. The actual *living* of things within the soul is Intuition. When it is said of Intuition that "through it man creeps into all things," this is literally true. — In ordinary life man has only one "intuition" — namely, of the ego itself, for the ego can in no way be perceived from without; it can only be experienced in the inner life. A simple consideration will make this fact clear. It is a consideration that has not been applied by psychologists with sufficient exactitude. Unimpressive as it may appear to one with full understanding, it is of the most far-reaching significance. It is as follows. A thing in the outer world can be called by all men by the self-same name. A table can be spoken of by all as a "table"; a tulip by all as a "tulip." Mr. Miller can be addressed by all as "Mr. Miller." But there is one word that each can apply only to himself. This is the word "I." No other person can call me "I." To anyone else I am a "you." In the same way everyone else is a "you" to me. Only I can say "I" to myself. This is because each man lives, not outside, but within the "I." In the same way, in intuitive cognition, one lives in

9

all things. The perception of the ego is the prototype of all intuitive cognition. Thus to enter into all things, one must first step outside oneself. One must become "selfless" in order to become blended with the "self," the "ego" of another being.

Meditation and concentration are the sure means by which to approach this stage of cognition, like the earlier ones. Of course, they must be practised in a quiet and patient way. Whoever supposes that he can violently, by forceful means, rise to higher worlds is mistaken. One giving himself over to such beliefs would be expecting the realities of the higher regions to meet him in the same way as those of the sensory world. Rich and vivid as are the worlds to which man may rise, yet they are delicate and subtle, while the world of sense is coarse and crude. The most important thing to be learned is that one must accustom oneself to regard as "real" something wholly different from what is so designated in the realm of sense. This is not easy. It is for this reason that so many who might willingly tread the occult path are frightened away at the first steps. Someone had expected to encounter things like tables and chairs, and instead finds "spirits." But since "spirits" are not like chairs and tables, they seem like "illusions." The only thing wrong is the unusualness. One must first acquire the right feeling for the spiritual world; then one will not only see, but also will acknowledge, what is spiritual. A great part of occult training is concerned with this right acknowledgment and assessment of the spiritual.

The state of sleep must first be considered to arrive at any understanding of imaginative cognition. As long as man has attained to no higher stage than material cognition, the soul truly lives during sleep, yet is incapable of perception in the world in which it dwells in the sleeping state. It is in this world like a blind man among material objects. Such a one lives in the world of light and color, but does not perceive them. — From the outer sense organs, the eye, the ear, the ordinary brain activity, and so forth, the soul has withdrawn in sleep. It receives no impressions through the senses. Now what is it doing during sleep? It must be realized that in waking life the soul is continually active. It takes in the outer sense impressions and works upon them. That is its activity. It stops this during sleep. But it is not idle. While sleeping, it works upon its own body. This body is worn out by the activity of the day. This expresses itself in fatigue. During sleep the soul occupies itself with its own body in order to prepare it for further work when it again awakens. We see from this how essential is proper sleep to bodily well-being. Accordingly, the man who does not sleep sufficiently hinders his soul in this necessary repair work upon the body. The consequence must be that the body deteriorates. The forces with which the soul works upon the body during sleep are the same through which it is active in the waking state. But in the latter case they are applied for absorbing the impressions of the outer senses and working upon them.

Now when imaginative cognition approaches in man, part of the forces directed upon the body in sleep must be employed in another way. Through these forces are formed the spiritual sense organs that provide the possibility for the soul not merely to live in a higher world, but also to perceive it. Thus the soul during sleep works no longer merely upon the body, but also upon itself. This work results from meditation and concentration, as well as from other exercises. It has often been stated in my writings about higher knowledge that the particular directions for such exercises are given only from one individual to another. No one should undertake such exercises on his own account. For only he who has experience in this realm can judge what effect comes about for one man or another who undertakes to withdraw his soul-work from the body and apply it in a higher way.

Meditation, concentration and other exercises bring it about that the soul withdraws for a time from its union with the sense organs. It is then immersed in itself. Its activity is turned inward. In the first stages of this self-immersion, its inner activity differs but little from its daily wont. In its inward labors, to be sure, it must make use of the self-same thoughts, feelings and sensations as belong to the habitual life. The more the soul accustoms itself to be in a measure "blind and deaf" to the material environment, the more it lives within itself, the better it fits itself for inward accomplishments. What is accomplished by the immersion in the inner life bears fruit first of all in the state of sleep. When at night the soul is freed from the body, what has been stimulated in it by the exercises of the day works on. Organs take shape within it, through which it comes into connection with a higher environment, exactly as through the outer sense organs it had formerly united itself with the corporeal world. Out of the darkness of nocturnal surroundings appear the light phenomena of the higher world. Tender and intimate at first is this communion. It must be taken into account in this connection that for a long time, upon awakening, the light of day will draw a dense veil over the night's experiences. The *recol-*

lection that perception has occurred during the night appears only slowly and gradually. For the student does not easily learn to pay attention to the delicate formations of his soul that in the course of his development begin to mingle with the common experiences of daily sense-life. At first, such formations of the soul resemble what are generally referred to as casual impressions. Everything depends upon his learning to distinguish what is due to the ordinary world from what through its own nature presents itself as a manifestation from higher worlds. In a quiet, introspective mental life he must acquire this discernment. It is necessary first to develop a sense of the value and meaning of those intimate formations of the soul that mingle themselves with daily life as though they were "chance impressions," but that are really recollections of the nightly communion with a higher world. As soon as one seizes these things in a crude way and applies to them the measuring stick of sensory life, they vanish.

It is evident from the foregoing that, through work in a higher world, the soul must withdraw from the body some of its activity ordinarily bestowed upon it with such care. It leaves the body to a certain extent self-dependent, and the body needs a substitute for what the soul had formerly done for it. If it does not obtain such a substitute, it comes in danger of mischief from hurtful forces, for one must in this regard be clear that man is continually subject to the influences of his surroundings. Actually he lives only through the influences of these surroundings. Among these, the kingdoms of visible nature first of all come under consideration. Man himself belongs to this visible nature. If there were no mineral, plant and animal kingdoms, nor other human beings around him, he could not live. If an individual could be imagined as cut off from the earth and lifted up into surrounding space, he would have to perish instantly as a physical being, just as the hand would wither if cut off from the body. Just as the illusion would be formidable if a human hand were to believe that it could exist without the body, so powerful would be the deception of a man who maintained that he could exist as a physical being without the mineral, vegetable and animal kingdoms, and without other men. — But besides the above-named kingdoms there are three others that generally escape the notice of man. These are the three elemental kingdoms. They stand, in a sense, below the mineral kingdom. There are beings who do not condense into the mineral condition, but who are none the less present and exert their influence upon man. (Further information concerning these elemental kindoms will be found in my *Cosmic Memory,* and also in the remarks about them in my *Theosophy.*) Man is thus exposed to influences from kingdoms of nature that in a sense must be called invisible. Now, when the soul works upon the body, a considerable part of its activity consists in regulating the influences of the elemental kingdoms in such a way that they are beneficial to man. — The instant the soul withdraws part of its activity from the body, injurious powers from the elemental kingdoms may get hold of it. Herein lies a danger of higher development. Therefore care must be taken that, as soon as the soul is withdrawn from the body, the latter is in itself accessible only to good influences from the elemental world. If this be disregarded, the ordinary man deteriorates, to a certain extent, physically and also morally, in spite of having gained access to higher worlds. While the soul dwells in the higher regions, pernicious forces insinuate themselves into the dense physical body and the etheric body. This is the reason why certain bad qualities, which before the higher development had been held in check by the regulating power of the soul, may now come to the fore for want of caution. Men formerly of good moral nature may, under such circumstances, when they enter higher worlds, reveal all kinds of low inclinations, increased selfishness, untruthfulness, vindictiveness, wrath, and so forth. — No one alarmed by this fact need be deterred from rising to the higher worlds, but care must be taken to prevent the occurrence of such things. The lower nature of man must be fortified and made inaccessible to dangerous elemental influences. This can be brought about by the conscious cultivation of certain virtues. These virtues are set forth in the writings on spiritual development. Here is the reason why they must be carefully sought after. They are the following.

First of all, the human being must, in a fully conscious manner, in all things, continually be intent upon the lasting, distinguish the imperishable from the transitory and turns his attention toward it. In all things and beings he can suppose or discern something that remains after the transitory appearance has faded away. If I see a plant, I can first observe it as it presents itself to the senses. No one should neglect to do this, for no one who has not first made himself thoroughly familiar with the perishable aspect will detect the eternal in things. Those who are continually afraid that to fix their attention on the spiritually imperishable will cause them to lose the freshness and naturalness of life do not really know what is being dealt with. But when I look at a plant in this way, it can become clear to me that there is in it a lasting living impulse that will reappear in a new plant when the present plant has long since crumbled to dust. Such an orientation toward things must be adopted in the whole temper of life. — Then the heart must be fixed upon all that is valuable and genuine, which one must learn to esteem more highly than the fleeting and insignificant. In all feelings and actions, the value of any single thing must be held before the eyes in the context of the whole. — Thirdly, six qualities should be developed: control of the thought world, control of actions, endurance, impartiality, trust in the surrounding world, and inner equilibrium. Control of the thought world can be attained if one takes the trouble to combat that wandering will-o'-the-wisping of the thoughts and feelings that in ordinary human beings are constantly rising and falling. In everyday life man is not the master of his thoughts; he is driven by them. Naturally, it cannot be otherwise, for life drives man and as a practical person he must yield to this. In ordinary life there is no alternative. But if a higher world is to be approached, at least brief periods must be set aside in which one makes oneself ruler of one's thought and feeling world. Therein, in complete inner freedom one puts a thought in the center of one's soul, where otherwise ideas obtrude themselves upon one from without. Then one tries to keep away all intruding thoughts and feeling and to link with the first thought only what one wills to admit as suitable. Such an exercise works beneficially upon the soul and through it also upon the body. It brings the latter into such a harmonious condition that it withdraws itself from injurious influences despite the fact that the soul is not directly acting upon it. — Control of actions consists of a similar regulation of these through inner freedom. A good beginning is made when one sets oneself to do regularly something that it would not have occurred to us to do in ordinary life. For in the latter, man is indeed driven to his actions from without. But the smallest action undertaken on one's innermost initiative accomplishes more in the direction indicated than all the pressures of outer life. — Endurance consists in holding oneself at a distance from every whim that can be designated as a shift from "exulting to the highest heaven to grieving even unto death." Man is driven to and fro among all kinds of moods. Pleasure makes him glad; pain depresses him. This has its justification. But he who seeks the path to higher knowledge must be able to mitigate joy and also grief. He must become stable. He must with moderation surrender to pleasurable impressions and also painful experiences; he must move with dignity through both. He must never be unmanned nor disconcerted. This does not produce lack of feeling, but it brings man to the steady center within the ebbing and flowing tide of life around him. He has himself always in hand.

Another important quality is the "yea saying" sense. This can be developed in one who in all things has an eye for the good, beautiful, and purposeful aspects of life, and not, primarily, for the blameworthy, ugly and contradictory. In Persian poetry there is a beautiful legend about Christ, which illustrates the meaning of this quality. A dead dog is lying on the road. Among the passersby is Christ. All the others turn away from the ugly sight; only Christ pauses and speaks admiringly of the animal's beautiful teeth. It is possible to look at things in this way, and he who earnestly seeks for it may find in all things, even the most repulsive, something worthy of acknowledgment.

The fruitfulness in things is not in what is lacking in them, but in what they have. — Further, it is important to develop the quality of "impartiality." Every human being has gone through his own experiences and has formed from them a fixed set of opinions according to which he directs his life. Just as conformity to experience is of course necessary, on the one hand, it is also important that he who would pass through spiritual development to higher knowledge should always keep an eye open for everything new and unfamiliar that confronts him. He will be as cautious as possible with judgments such as, "That is impossible," "That cannot be." Whatever opinion he may have formed from previous experiences, he will be ready at any moment, when he encounters something new, to admit a new opinion. All love of one's own opinion must vanish. — When the five above mentioned qualities have been acquired, a sixth then presents itself as a matter of course: Inner balance, the harmony of the spiritual forces. The human being must find within himself a spiritual center of gravity that gives him firmness and security in the face of all that would pull him hither and thither in life. The sharing in all surrounding life must not be shunned, and everything must be allowed to work upon one. Not flight from all the distracting activities of life is the correct course, but rather, the full devoted yielding to life, *along with* the sure, firm guarding of inner balance and harmony.

Lastly, the "will to freedom," must come within the seeker's consideration. Whoever finds within himself the support and basis of all that he accomplishes already has this attribute. It is so hard to achieve because of the balance necessary between the opening of the senses to everything great and good and the simultaneous rejection of every compulsion. It is so easy to say that influence from without is incompatible with freedom. The essential thing is that the two should be reconciled within the soul. When someone tells me something and I accept it under the compulsion of his authority, I am not free. But I am no less unfree if I shut myself off from the good that I might receive in this way. For then worse elements in my own soul act as a compulsion upon me. Freedom means not only that I am free from the compulsion of an outside authority, but above all that I am not subservient to any prejudices, opinions, sensations and feelings of my own. The right way is not blind subjection to what is received, but to leave ourselves open to suggestion, receiving it impartially, so that we may freely acknowledge it. An outside authority should exert no more influence than to make one say, "I make myself free just by following the good in it — that is to say, by making it my own." An authority based upon occult wisdom will not at all exert influence otherwise than in this way. It gives whatever it has to give, not in order itself to gain power over the recipient, but solely that through the gift the recipient may become richer and freer.

The significance of the above-mentioned qualities has already been touched on in the discussion of the "lotus flowers."* Therein was shown their relation to the development of the twelve petalled lotus flower in the region of the heart, and to the currents of the etheric body connected with it. From what has been said it is now evident that these qualities enable the seeker to dispense with those

---

* Rudolf Steiner, *Knowledge of the Higher Worlds and Its Attainment,* Anthroposophic Press, Inc.

forces that formerly benefited the physical body during sleep, and which now, because of his development, must be gradually withdrawn from this task. Under such influences Imaginative Knowledge develops.

IMAGINATION

I T IS IMPOSSIBLE to make real progress in penetrating to the higher worlds without going through the stage of imaginative knowledge. This by no means implies that during occult training the human being is compelled to remain for a certain time at the imaginative stage as though it were something like a class to be attended at school. In certain instances this may be necessary, but by no means as a general rule. It depends entirely upon what the occult student has experienced before entering upon his occult training. It will be shown in the course of this discussion that the spiritual environment of the occult student is important in this regard, and that depending on his orientation to this spiritual environment diverse methods have been instituted for treading the path of knowledge.

It can be of the utmost importance to know what follows if one is preparing to undergo occult training. Not merely as an interesting theory does this come into consideration, but as something by which manifold practical points of view can be gained if one is to succeed on the "path to higher knowledge."

It is often said by those striving toward a higher development: I wish to perfect myself spiritually; I wish to develop the "higher man" within me; but I have no desire for the manifestations of the "astral world." This is understandable when one takes into consideration the descriptions of the astral world found in books dealing with such things. There, to be sure, appearances and beings are

21

spoken of that bring all sorts of dangers to men. It will be said that under the influence of such beings, a man may easily suffer harm to his moral disposition and mental health. It will be brought home to the reader that in these regions the wall dividing "the good from the evil path" is as "a spider's web" in thickness, and that the plunge into immeasurable abysses, the fall into utter depravity, lies all too near. — It is, of course, impossible simply to contradict such assertions. Yet the standpoint taken in many cases as to treading the occult path is in no way a correct one. The only reasonable point of view is the one that says, rather, that no one should be deterred from travelling the way of higher knowledge because of dangers, but that in every case strict care must be taken to weather these dangers. It may happen that one who asks an occult teacher's guidance will be counselled to postpone actual training for a time, and first undergo certain experiences of ordinary life or learn things that can be learned in the physical world. It will then be the task of the occult teacher to give the seeker the right instructions for accumulating such experiences and learning such things. In most cases, by far, the occult teacher will be found to proceed in this way. If then the student now is sufficiently attentive to what happens to him, after he has come into contact with the occult teacher, he will be able to observe many things. He will find that henceforth things happen to him as if "by accident," and that he can observe things that he would never have been exposed to without this link with the occult teacher. If the student does not notice this and becomes impatient, it is because he has not paid sufficient attention to what has happened to him. It is not to be believed that the influence of the teacher upon the student will show itself in distinctly visible "tricks of magic." This influence is rather an intimate matter, and he who would explore its nature and essence without having first reached a certain stage of occult training will surely err. The student injures himself in every case in which he becomes impatient over the waiting time prescribed for him. His advance will be none the less rapid on this account. On the contrary, his progress would be slowed down if he were to begin too soon the training he often impatiently awaits.

If the student allows the waiting time or the other advice and hints given to him by the occult teacher to influence him rightly, he will be actually preparing himself to hold his ground before certain trials and dangers that approach him when he encounters the unavoidable stage of Imagination. This stage is unavoidable for this reason: Everyone who seeks communication with the higher world without having passed through it can only do so unconsciously and is condemned to grope in the dark. One can acquire some dim sense of this higher world without Imagination; one can without it certainly attain to a sense of being united with "one's God" or "one's higher self," but one cannot in this way come to a true knowledge in full consciousness and bright, luminous clarity. Therefore, all talk about coming to terms with the "inferior spiritual worlds" (the astral and the devachanic) being unnecessary, that the one thing needful is for man to awaken the God within him," is no more than illusion. — Whoever is satisfied with this approach should not be interfered with in his strivings, and the occultist would not so interfere. But true occultism has nothing at all to do with such strivings. It makes no demand upon anybody to become a

23

pupil. But in him who seeks its discipline it will awaken no mere dim perception of himself as "godlike," but will also try to open his spiritual eyes to what actually exists in higher worlds.

Of course, the "divine self" is contained in every man. It is in every created being. In stone, plant, and animal, the "divine self" is also contained and active. But it does not so much matter to feel and know this in general as to enter into a living connection with the *manifestations* of this "divine self." Just as one can mutter over and over again that this world contains the "divine self" veiled within it and know nothing thereby of the physical world, so does he who seeks the "divine kingdom of spirits" only in blurred and indeterminate generalities know nothing of higher worlds. One should open the eyes and *behold* the revelation of deity in the things of the physical world, in the stone, in the plant, and not merely dream away all these as only "appearances" with the true form of God somehow "concealed" behind them. No, God reveals Himself in His creations, and whoever would know God must learn to know the true essence of these creations. Therefore one must also learn to behold what really goes on and is living in the higher worlds, if one would know the "divine." The consciousness that the "God-man" dwells within one can at most provide a beginning. But this beginning experienced in the right way, rises to an actual lift into the higher worlds. But this is possible only for one in whom the spiritual "senses" have been developed. Any other view arrives only at the standpoint, "I will stay as I am and attain only what is possible for me to attain in this way." But the aim of the occultist is to become a different human being, in order to behold and experience other things than the customary ones.

It is precisely for this purpose that passage through imaginative knowledge is necessary. It has already been said that this stage of Imagination need not be conceived of as a school class that must be gone through. It is to be understood that, particularly in present-day life, there are persons who bring with them pre-conditions enabling the occult teacher to call forth in them inspired and intuitive knowledge simultaneously, or nearly so, with the imaginative. But it is not at all to be understood that any person could be spared passage through the imaginative stage.

The cause of danger inherent in imaginative knowledge has already been pointed out in my book, *Knowledge of the Higher Worlds and Its Attainment*. This cause is that upon entrance into that world the human being in a certain sense loses the ground under his feet. The source of his security in the physical world is for the moment to all appearances entirely lost. Upon perception of something in the physical world it is asked: Whence comes this perception? This is mostly done unconsciously. But it is quite "unconsciously" clear that the causes of the perception are objects "outside in space." Colors, sounds, odors go out from these objects. Colors would not be seen floating free in space, nor sounds heard, without consciousness arising as to the objects to which these colors pertain as qualities, and from which these tones come. This consciousness that objects and entities cause physical perceptions gives to them, and thereby to man himself, his security and sure hold. Anyone having perceptions without outward causes is spoken of as abnormal and morbid. Such causeless perceptions are called illusions, hallucinations, visions.

Now first of all, viewed entirely outwardly, the whole imaginative world consists of such hallucinations, visions, and illusions. It has been pointed out* how, through occult training, such visions, etc., are artificially produced. By focusing the consciousness on a seed or a dying plant, certain forms, which to begin with are nothing but hallucinations, are conjured up before the soul. The "flame-formation," spoken of as appearing in the soul through observation of a plant or the like, and that after a time completely separates itself from the plant, is, outwardly viewed, to be regarded on the same level as an hallucination. It is the same in occult training when the imaginative world is entered. What was customarily regarded as going forth from things "outside in space," or "clinging to them" as properties — colors, sounds, odors, etc., — now float free in space. Perceptions break loose from all outer things and swim free in space, or fly around in it. Yet it is known with strict accuracy that the things before us have not brought forth these perceptions, but rather that they are self-induced by the human being. So it is that one thinks one has "lost the ground under one's feet." In ordinary life in the physical world those inner picturings that do not proceed from things must be guarded against and are without ground or foundation. But to call forth imaginative knowledge, the prime essential is to have colors, sounds, odors, etc., fully torn loose from all things, "floating free in space."

---

*See: *Knowledge of the Higher Worlds and Its Attainment*

The next step towards imaginative knowledge is to find a new "ground and foundation" for the picturings that are thus adrift. This must occur in that other world that is now about to be revealed. New things and entities take possessions of these inner picturings. In the physical world, for instance, the color blue stays on a cornflower. In the imaginative world likewise it must not remain "free-floating." It streams, as it were, towards some being, and whereas it floated unattached at first, it now becomes the expression of a being. Something speaks through it that the observer can only perceive in the imaginative world, and so these "free-floating" picturings gather around definite centers. It becomes clear that beings are speaking to us through them. And, as in the physical world there are corporeal things and beings to which colors, sounds, odors, and so forth, are attached or from which they are derived, so now spiritual beings speak out through them. These "spiritual beings" are, in fact, always there; they hover continually around human beings. But they cannot reveal themselves to them if the occasion is not given them to do so. They are given this opportunity when one calls forth the capacity to let sounds, colors, and so forth, arise before one's soul, even when occasioned by no physical object.

The "spiritual facts and beings" are entirely different from the objects and entities of the physical world. In ordinary speech it is not easy to find an expression that even remotely describes this difference. Perhaps it can best be approached by saying that in the imaginative world everything speaks to man as if it were directly intelligent, whereas in the physical world intelligence can only reveal itself in a roundabout way through corporeality. Exactly this makes for mobility and freedom in the imaginative world — that the medium of the outer object is missing, and the spiritual lives itself out with full immediacy in the free-floating tones, colors, etc.

Now the basis of danger threatening the human being in this world lies in the fact that he perceives the manifestations of "spiritual beings," but not the beings themselves. This is the case as long as he remains only in the imaginative world and rises no higher. Only Inspiration and intuition lead him gradually to the beings themselves. — If, however, the occult teacher should awaken these faculties permaturely, without having thoroughly introduced the pupil to the realm of Imagination, the higher world would have for him only a shadowy and phantasmal existence. The whole glorious fullness of the pictures in which it must reveal itself when one really enters into it, would be lost. Herein lies the reason why the occult student needs a "guide."

For the student, the imaginative world is at first only a "picture world" of which mostly he does not know the meaning. But the occult teacher knows to what things and entities these pictures pertain in a still higher world. If the student has confidence in him, he can know that later connections will be revealed to him, which he cannot yet penetrate. In the physical world, the objects in space were themselves his guides. He was in a position to prove the accuracy of his inner picturings of them. The corporeal reality is the "rock" upon which all hallucinations and illusions must be shattered. This rock disappears into an abyss when the imaginative world is entered. Therefore the teacher must serve as another such rock. From what he is able to offer, the student must sense the reality of the new world. From this it can be judged what great confidence in the teacher must exist in any occult training worthy of the name. When he can no longer believe in the teacher, it is exactly the same in this higher world as if in the physical world everything on which his faith in the reality of his perceptions had been built were suddenly taken from him.

Apart from this fact, there is yet another through which the human being might be thrown into confusion if he were to enter the imaginative world without guidance, for the occult student has in the first place to learn to know *himself* as distinct from all other spiritual beings. In physical life man has feelings, desires, longings, passions, ideas, and so forth. True, these are all caused by things and beings of the outer world, but the human being knows quite definitely that they form his inner world, and he distinguishes them from the objects of the outer world as what is happening within his soul. But as soon as the imaginative sense is awakened, this ease of differentiation completely ceases. His own feelings, ideas, passions, and so forth, literally step outside him and take on form, color and tone. He stands before them now as before wholly strange objects and beings in the physical world. It will be understood that the confusion can become complete if it is remembered what has been said in the chapter, "Some Results of Initiation," in my book, *Knowledge of the Higher Worlds and Its Attainment.* The way in which the imaginative world appears to the observer is described there. All appears there reversed as in a reflected image. What streams out from man appears as if it were coming toward him from outside. A wish that he cherishes changes into a shape — for example, into the form of some fantastic looking animal, or again into an entity resembling a human being. This appears to assail him, to make an attack on him, or to cause him to do this or that. So it can happen that the human being appears to himself as surrounded by a wholly fantastic, often charming and seductive, often also horrible, world of fluttering forms. In reality these are nothing other than his thoughts, wishes, and passions, transformed into images. — It would be a great error to believe it easy to distinguish between this self transformed into images on the one hand and the real spiritual world on the other. At first it is downright impossible for the student to make this distinction. For the identical picture can come from some spiritual being that speaks to men or from something in the interior of the soul, and if one's development is unduly precipitate at this point, there is danger of never learning to separate the two in an orderly fashion. The greatest caution is to be the rule in this regard. — Now the confusion will be still greater in that the wishes and desires of the soul clothe themselves in images of an exactly opposite character from what they really are. It may be assumed, for instance, that vanity clothes itself in a picture in this way. It may appear as a charming shape promising the most wonderful things if its dictates are carried out. Its pronouncements seem to set goals thoroughly good and worth striving for; if followed, they plunge one into moral and other kinds of ruin. Conversely, a good soul quality can clothe itself in unprepossessing garb. At this point only the real knower can differentiate, and only a personality unsusceptible to weakening in respect to a right aim is steady in face of the seductive artifices of his own soul's imagery. — From these considerations it will be recognized how necessary is the guidance of a teacher who, with a sure sense, makes the pupil attentive to what in this realm is phantasm and what is truth. There is no need to believe that the teacher must always stand just behind the pupil. The presence of the teacher close to the occult student in space is not what matters most. Certainly there is the moment when such spatial presence is desirable, and also when it is absolutely necessary. But on the other hand, the occult teacher finds means of remaining in touch with the pupil even when spatially far removed. Besides, it must be observed that much of what takes place between teacher and pupil in this sphere when they meet can go on working often for months and perhaps for years afterward. But there is one thing that must surely destroy the necessary link between teacher and pupil. This happens if the pupil loses confidence in the teacher.— It is particularly bad if this bond of confidence is broken before the pupil has learned to distinguish the illusory reflections of his own soul from true reality.

Now it could perhaps at this point be argued that if a connection with the teacher occurs in this way, the occult student loses all freedom and independence. He gives himself, so to speak, wholly into the hands of the teacher. This is in truth, however, not at all the case. The various methods of occult training certainly differ from one another with respect to this dependence upon the teacher. This dependence can be required to be a greater or a lesser one. It is relatively greatest in the method that was followed by the Oriental occultists, and even today is taught by them as their own. This dependence is already proportionately less in the so-called Christian initiation, and, properly speaking, its complete omission comes on the path of knowledge that, since the fourteenth century, has come to be advanced by the so-called Rosicrucian occult schools. On this path the teacher can by no means be disregarded; that is impossible. But all dependence on him ceases. How this is possible will be presented in the continuation of these thoughts hereafter. Therein we shall explain precisely how these three paths of knowledge differ: the oriental, the Christian, and the Rosicrucian. In the Rosicrucian approach there is nothing at all upsetting in any way to a modern man's sense of freedom. It will also be described in this continuation how one person or another as an occult student, even in present-day Europe, may travel, not the Rosicrucian, but the Oriental path, or the old Christian; although today the Rosicrucian is the most natural. This way, as will be seen in due course, is not at all unchristian. A man can go this way without endangering his Christianity, as can also he who supposes himself to stand at the pinnacle of the modern scientific world-conception.

But perhaps one other explanation is needed. One might feel tempted to ask whether the occult student could not be spared going through the delusions of his own soul. But if this happened, he would never attain to that independent discernment so desirable for him. For by no other means can the singular nature of the imaginative world be so well grasped as by the observation of one's own soul. To begin with, man knows the inner life of his soul from one side. He is immersed in it, and this is just what the occult student has to learn — not only to look at things from outside, but to observe them as if he himself were within all of them. If his own thought world now meets him as something foreign, and he already knows a thing from one side, he can still learn to know it from another. He must himself become to a certain extent the first example of such knowledge. Here in the physical world he is accustomed to something quite different. Here he looks upon all other things only from outside, but he experiences himself only from the inside. As long as he remains in the physical world, he can never see behind the surface of things. He can never go outside himself, "slip out of his skin," as it were, to observe *himself* from outside. This objective observation of himself is literally his first obligation in occult training, this helps him learn also to look beneath the surface of outer facts and beings.

INSPIRATION

FROM THE DESCRIPTION of Imagination it has become evident how through it the occult student leaves the ground of outer sense experiences. In a much higher degree is this the case with Inspiration. Here representation (image forming) is based much less upon what can be designated an outer stimulus. Man must find strength within himself to make it possible for him to form representations concerning things. He must be inwardly active on a much higher level than in the case of outer cognition. There he simply gives himself over to outer impressions, and these cause the images. This kind of surrender ceases when we come to Inspiration. No eye any longer supplies colors, no ear supplies sounds, and so forth. The whole content of representations must largely be shaped by one's own activity, consequently by purely spirit-soul processes, and the manifestation of the higher world must be impressed upon what man has created by his inner activity. A peculiar contradiction seems to appear in such a description of the world of higher cognition. The individual to a certain extent should be the creator of his own representations yet of course these representations must not be allowed to be his own creation. The processes of the higher world must be expressed through them just as the processes of the lower world are expressed through the perceptions of the eyes, ears, and so forth. But a contradition is inevitable in the description of this mode of cognition, for this is exactly what the occult student must make his own on the path of Inspiration; he must attain by his inner activity a result that in ordinary life is outwardly compelled. — Why in ordinary life do the images representing the outer world not take their course arbitrarily? Because man has to make his inner imagery conform to the outer objects. All arbitrariness of the "ego" falls away because the objects say: We are that, or that. The objects themselves tell how they shall be thought of; the "ego" has nothing to decide about it. Whoever will not adjust himself to the objects has erroneous thoughts, and he would soon become aware of how little success he would have with them in the world. This necessary attitude of human beings to the things of the outer world can be designated in cognition by the term "selfless." Man must attain a "selfless" attitude toward things, and the outer world is his instructor in this selflessness. It removes from him all illusions, all fantastic notions, all illogical judgments, all non-objectivity, simply by putting the correct image before his senses.

If the human being wants to prepare himself for Inspiration, he must so develop his inner nature that this selflessness is his very own, even when nothing outside compels it. He must learn to create inwardly, but in such a way that his "ego" does not in the least way play an arbitrary role in this creative activity. The difficulties to be considered in achieving such selflessness become the more apparent the more consideration is given to what soul powers are especially needed for Inspiration.—The three fundamental powers of soul life are differentiated: Representation (thinking), feeling, and willing. In every-day sensory cognition, representations are stimulated into existence by outer objects, and through these externally stimulated representations the directions taken by feeling and willing are determined. For instance, the human being sees an object; it gives him pleasure, and in consequence he desires the things concerned. Pleasure is rooted in feeling, and through feeling the will is aroused, just as feeling has itself received its stamp from thinking. But the ultimate foundation of thinking, feeling and willing is the external object. — Another instance would be this. A man witnesses an event. It frightens him. He runs away from the scene of the event. Here, too, the outer occurrences are the initial cause; they are perceived through the senses, become representations, the feeling of fear springs up; and the will — expressing itself in running away — is the result. In Inspiration any outer object of this kind falls away. The senses do not come into play for a perception. Therefore they cannot give rise to representations. From this side no influence is exerted upon feeling and willing. Yet it is precisely from these two, as out of a mother substance, that in Inspiration representations inwardly arise and grow. If the mother substance is healthy, true representations will arise; if unhealthy, errors and illusions.

As certainly as inspirations that originate in healthy feeling and willing can be revelations from a higher world, so certainly do errors, delusions and fantastic notions concerning a higher world spring from confused feeling and willing.

Occult training therefore undertakes to indicate how the human being may make his feelings and his will impulses productive in a healthy way for Inspiration. As in all matters of occult training, the need here is for an *intimate* regulating and forming of soul life. First of all certain feelings must be developed which are known only to a slight degree in ordinary life. Some of these feelings will be hinted at here. Among the most important is a heightened sensitiveness to "truth" and "falsehood," to "right" and "wrong." Certainly the ordinary human being has similar feelings, but they must be developed by the occult student in a much higher measure. Suppose someone has made a logical error. Another sees this mistake and corrects it. Let it be clear how great is the role of judgment and intellect in such a correction, and how slight the feeling of pleasure in the right and displeasure in the wrong. Surely this is not to claim that the pleasure and corresponding displeasure are non-existent. But the degree to which they are present in ordinary life must be illimitably raised in occult training. Most systematically must the occult student turn his attention to his soul life, and he must bring it about that logical error is a source of pain to him, no less excruciating than physical pain, and conversely, that the "right" gives him real joy and delight. Thus, where another only stirs his intellect, his power of judgment, into motion, the occult student must learn to live through the whole gamut of emotions, from grief to enthusiasm, from afflictive tension to transports of delight in the possession of truth. In fact, he must learn to feel something like hatred against what the "normal" man experiences only in a cold and sober way as "incorrect"; he must enkindle in himself a love of truth that bears a personal character; as personal, as warm, as the lover feels for the beloved. — Certainly much is spoken in our "cultured" circles about the "love of truth" yet what is meant by this is not at all to be compared with what the occult student must go through in quiet, inner

37

soul work toward this end. As a test, he must patiently, over and over again, place before himself this or that "true" thing, this or that "false" one, and devote himself to it, not merely to train his power of judgment for sober discrimination between "true" and "false," but he must gain an entirely personal relation to it all. — It is absolutely correct that at the beginning of such training the human being can fall into what may be called "oversensitiveness." An incorrect judgment that he hears in his environment, an inconsistency, and so forth, can cause him almost unbearable pain. — Care must therefore be taken in this respect during training. Otherwise great dangers might indeed result for the student's equilibrium of soul. If care is taken that the character remains steadfast, storms may occur in the soul life and the human being still retain the power to conduct himself toward the outer world with harmonious countenance and bearing. A mistake is made in every case in which the occult student is brought into opposition to the outer world so that he finds it unbearable or wishes to flee from it entirely. The higher world of feeling must not be cultivated at the expense of well-balanced activity and work in the outer world; therefore a strengthening of the power to withstand outer impressions must appear in corresponding measure to the inner lifting of the feeling life. Practical occult training, therefore, directs the human being never to undertake the above-mentioned exercises for developing the feeling world without at the same time developing himself toward an appreciation of the tolerance that life demands from men. He must be able to feel the keenest pain if a person utters an erroneous opinion, and yet at the same time be perfectly tolerant towards this person because the thought in his mind is equally clear that this person is bound to judge in this way, and his opinion must be reckoned with as a fact. — It is, of course, correct that the inner being of the occult scientist will be ever more and more transformed into a twofold life. Ever richer processes come about in his soul in his pilgrimage through life, and a second world becomes continually more independent of what the outer world offers. It is just this twofold existence that will bear fruit in the genuine practice of life. What results from it is quick-witted judgment and unerring certainty of decision. While anyone who stands remote from such schooling must go through long trains of thought, driven hither and thither between resolution and perplexity, the occult scientist will swiftly survey life situations and discern hidden relations concealed from the ordinary view. He then often needs much patience to synchronize with the slow rate at which another person is able to grasp something that for him comes swift as an arrow.

Thus far we have spoken only of the qualities that must be developed in the feeling life so that Inspiration may occur in the correct way. The next question is: How do the feelings become fruitful so that they are accurately represented for the world of Inspiration? If one wishes to understand what occult science has to offer in answer to this question, acquaintance is necessary with the fact that man's soul life has always a certain treasure of feeling over and above those stimulated by sense perceptions. The human being feels, as it were, far more than things compel him to feel, only in ordinary life this excess is employed in a direction that through occult training must be transformed into another. Take, for instance, a feeling of anxiety or fear. It can be crystal clear that often fear or anxiety is greater than it would be if it were in true proportion to the corresponding outer event. Imagine that the occult student is working energetically on himself with the aim to feel in no instance more fear and anxiety than is justified by the corresponding external events. Now a given amount of fear or anxiety always entails an expenditure of soul force. This soul force is actually lost as a result when fear or anxiety is produced. The student really conserves this soul force when he denies himself fear or anxiety — or other such feelings — and it remains at his disposal for some other purpose. If he repeats such processes often, he will build up an inner treasure of these continually husbanded soul forces, and the occult student will soon find that out of such economies of feeling will arise the germs of those inner images that will bring to expression the revelations of a higher life. Such things cannot be "proved" in the ordinary sense; the occult student can only be advised to do this or that, and if he does so to watch for the indubitable results.

A careless examination of what has been described might easily make it appear as a contradiction to demand from the one side an enrichment of the feeling world, with feelings of pleasure or pain to be kindled by what otherwise arouses only intellectual judgment, and from the other side to talk in almost the same breath of economy of feeling. This contradiction quickly disappears if it is borne in mind that the economies are to be effected in those feelings aroused by the outer senses. Just what is conserved there appears conversely as an enrichment of spiritual experience, and it is wholly correct that the feelings conserved in this way in the world of sense perception not only become free in the other sphere, but prove *creative* in that sphere. — They shape the matrix substance for those representations wherein the spiritual world reveals itself.

But it would not accomplish much to remain at a standstill with only such economies as those indicated above. For greater results, still more is necessary. A far greater treasure still of power to create feeling must be supplied to the soul than is possible in this way alone. For instance, as a test, one must expose oneself to certain outer impressions, and then wholly deny oneself the feelings that "normally" arise as a result. One must, for instance, face an occurrence that "normally" excites the soul, and absolutely and totally forbid oneself the excitation. This can be accomplished either by actually confronting such an experience, or by conjuring it up imaginatively. The imaginative method is even better for a really fruitful occult training. As the student is initiated into Imagination, either before his preparation for Inspiration or simultaneously with it, he should actually be in a position to place an occurrence imaginatively before the soul with the same force as if it were in fact taking place. — If, therefore, in the course of long inner work the student ever again and again subjects himself to things and events, yet denies himself the corresponding "normal" feelings, a fertile ground for Inspiration will be created in his soul. — Just incidentally it might be noted here that he who is describing such training for Inspiration can fully appreciate possible objections against such a description from the standpoint of present-day culture. Not only can objections be made, but people may smile haughtily and say, "Inspiration cannot be pedantically taught; it is a natural gift of genius." Yes, from the standpoint of modern culture, it may certainly seem almost comical to

41

speak of a process that this culture will not admit to be explainable, but this culture is itself not conscious of how little it is able to think through its own thought processes to the end. Whoever would expect a disciple of this culture to believe that some more highly developed animal had not slowly evolved, but had appeared "suddenly," would soon hear that a person cultured in the modern sense would not believe in such a "miracle." Such a belief would be "superstition." Now in the sphere of soul life, one with such modern education is himself but the victim of crass superstition simply in the style of his own opinions. By the same token, he will not recognize that a more fully developed soul must also have evolved, that it could not have sprung into existence suddenly as a gift of nature. Of course, externally, many a genius appears to have been born suddenly "out of nothing" in some mysterious way; but it appears so only for materialistic superstition; the spiritual scientist knows that the assessment of genius with respect to the life of a man born to this condition as if out of nothing is simply the result of his preparation for Inspiration during an earlier life on earth. — In the theoretical sphere, materialistic superstition is bad, but it is still worse in the practical sphere such as is concerned here. As it assumes that genius in the whole of the future must "fall from heaven," it does not trouble itself about this "occult nonsense" or "fantastic mysticism" that speaks of preparation for Inspiration. In this way the superstition of the materialists retards the true progress of mankind. It does not see to it that the latent faculties are developed in man.

In reality, precisely those who call themselves progressives and free-thinkers are often the enemies of true progress. But this, as noted, is but a casual remark, necessary because of the relationship of occult science to present-day culture.

Now the soul powers that are stored up in the student's inner being by self-denial of "normal" feelings, as indicated above, are riches that would undoubtedly be transformed into Inspirations even if nothing else came to their aid, and the occult student would experience how true thought images arise in his soul, representing experiences in higher worlds. Progress would begin with the simplest experiences of supersensible events, and slowly more complicated and higher ones appear, if the student continued to live inwardly according to the suggested directions. — But in reality such occult training today would be entirely impractical, and nowhere is it carried out where work is undertaken earnestly. For, if the student wished to develop "out of himself" everything that Inspiration can give, he could undoubtedly "spin out" of himself all that has been said here, for example, about the nature of man, human life after death, the evolution of humanity and of the planets, and so forth. But such a student would need an immeasurably long time to do it. It would be, for example, as if a man would spin the whole of geometry out of himself, without regard for what had already been achieved in this realm before him. Certainly, in theory, it is fully possible. To carry it out in practice would be folly. Also, this is not the procedure in occult science, but through a teacher things are handed down that have been acquired for humanity by inspired predecessors. This tradition must for the present provide the basis for individual Inspiration. What is being offered today in literature and lectures out of the realm of occult science

43

can absolutely provide such a basis for Inspiration. There are, for example, the teachings about the various component parts of man (physical body, ether body, astral body, and so forth), the knowledge concerning life after death pending a new incarnation, and everything that has been printed under the title, *Cosmic Memory*. In other words, it must be held fast at all points that Inspiration is needed for discovering and personally experiencing the higher truths, but not for understanding them. What is communicated in *Cosmic Memory* cannot at first be discovered without Inspiration. But once communicated, then it can be understood through wholly ordinary logical judgment. No one should assert that things are stated there that cannot be logically grasped without Inspiration. They are found inconceivable, not because of lack of Inspiration, but because they are not given sufficient reflective consideration. — If such communicated truths are received, they awaken Inspiration in the soul through their own strength. If sharing in such Inspiration is desired, however, the effort must be made not to receive this knowledge in a prosaic and matter-of-fact way, but to open oneself to be moved by the upswing of ideas into all possible feeling experiences. Why should this not be possible? Can feeling remain dull when overpowering cosmic occurrences pass before the spirit's gaze — how the Earth has developed out of Moon, Sun, and Saturn, or when the infinite depths of human nature are penetrated by a knowledge of man's ether and astral bodies, and so forth? One might almost say, "How regrettable," for a person who can contemplate unmoved such edifices of thought. For if he did not regard them prosaically, but lived through all the tensions and relaxations of feeling that they make possible, all climaxes and crises, all progress and retrogression, all catastrophes and dispensions, then indeed would the mother substance be prepared in him for Inspiration itself. Certainly the necessary feeling life in the face of such communications from a higher world can be really unfolded only by exercises like those indicated above. Whoever turns all his feeling forces toward the outer world of sense perception will see narrations from a higher world as "arid concepts," as "gray theory." He will never be able to grasp why another finds the communications of occult science heartwarming, while his own heart remains cold to them. He will even say, "But this is only for the intellect; this is intellectual. I would like something for my whole well-being." But he does not tell himself that it is his own fault if his heart remains cold.

Many still undervalue the power of what lies already hidden in just these communications from a higher world, and in this connection they overvalue all kinds of other exercises and procedures. "What good is it to me," they say, "to learn from others what the higher worlds look like? I want to see them for myself." Such persons mostly lack the patience to concentrate over and over again upon such narrations from higher worlds. If they would do so, they would see what kindling force these "mere stories" have, and how one's own Inspiration is stimulated by hearing an account of the Inspirations of others. — Certainly other exercises must supplement mere "learning" if the student wishes to make rapid progress in the experience of the higher worlds, but no one should under-estimate the great significance precisely of "learning." In any case no hope can be given that he will make rapid conquests in the higher worlds through any exercises whatever, unless he has at the same time set out to ponder incessantly upon the communications, purely narrative, that have been given from a competent quarter about the events and beings of the higher worlds. — Now that such communications are actually being presented in literature and in lectures, and so forth, and the first indications are also being given for the exercises leading to knowledge of higher worlds (as, for example, such indications as are presented in *Knowledge of the Higher Worlds and Its Attainment*), it has now become possible to learn something of what formerly was communicated only in strictly guarded occult schools. As has been frequently mentioned, it is owing to the special conditions of our time that these things are and must be published. But also, on the other hand, it must be ever again emphasized that while it has thus been made easier to acquire occult knowledge, sure guidance through an experienced occult teacher is not yet to be completely dispensed with.

Cognition through Inspiration leads men to the experience of processes in the invisible worlds, as, for instance, the evolution of man and that of the earth and its planetary embodiments. But when in these higher worlds not only processes, but being come under consideration, then must Intuition enter in as a mode of cognition. What occurs through such being is discerned through Imagination in pictures; laws and relationships, through Inspiration; if one would come face to face with the beings themselves, Intuition is needed. — How Inspiration becomes articulate in the world of Imaginations, how it permeates the latter as a "spiritual music" and so becomes the means of expression for the beings who are to be known through Intuition, will be explained later. Then also Intuition itself will be

46

dealt with. Here it will merely be pointed out that what is designated as "Intuition" in occult science has nothing to do with the application of the word "intuition" in current popular usage. By this application is meant a more or less uncertain notion in contrast to clear cognition, logically arrived at through intellect or reason. In occult science, Intuition is nothing vague and uncertain, but a lofty mode of cognition, full of the most luminous clarity and the most indubitable certainty.

INSPIRATION AND INTUITION

J UST AS IMAGINATION may be called a spiritual *seeing,* so may Inspiration be called a spiritual *hearing.* Of course, it must be quite clear that by the expression "hearing" is meant a perception still further removed from sensory-hearing in the physical world than "sight" in the imaginative (astral) world is removed from seeing with the physical eyes. It can be said of the imaginative world's light and color phenomena that the radiant surfaces and colors of sensory-objects are as if lifted from these objects and released from them to float free in space. But this gives only an approximate idea, for "space" in the imaginative world is in no way like it is in the physical. Whoever fancies that he has before him imaginative color-pictures when he is seeing freely floating colored particles in ordinary space dimension is in error. — But the forming of such color representations is, nevertheless, the way to the imaginative life. Whoever tries to put a flower before his mind's-eye, and then separates off from his picture everything that does not represent color, so that an image of the colored surface, separate from the flower, is suspended before his soul, can gradually through such exercises arrive at an Imagination. This picture itself is not yet such Imagination, but is more or less preliminary fantasy suggestion. Imagination, that is, the real astral experience first exists when not only the color is wholly lifted apart from the sense impression, but when also the three-dimensional space has fully lost itself. That this is the case can be confirmed only

48

by a certain feeling. This feeling is described by saying that one no longer feels oneself "outside" but "inside" the color-picture and has the consciousness of partaking of its coming into being. If this feeling is not there, if one remains standing before the thing as before a sense-bound color-picture, then one has to do, not yet with real Imagination, but with something of the fanciful. It should not be said that such fantasy pictures are wholly worthless. They can actually be etheric reflections — like shadows — of real astral facts. As such they have their own value in occult-scientific training. They can form a bridge to true astral (imaginative) experiences. — A certain danger lurks in the observation only if the observer does not fully apply his sound human judgment at this frontier between the sensible and the supersensible. It is not to be expected that an unfailing test can be given whereby at this frontier he can differentiate illusion, hallucination, and the fantastic from reality. Such a general rule would surely be comfortable. But comfort is a word that the occult student should strike from his vocabulary. — It can only be said that he who would acquire clarity of discernment in this sphere must already be intent upon it in the ordinary life of the physical world. Whoever takes no care in ordinary life to think sharply and clearly will fall a victim to all possible illusions on his ascent into higher worlds. It has only to be considered how many snares of everyday life beset sound judgment. How often human beings do not see in an unconfused way what exists, but rather what they crave to see! In how many cases do men believe something, not because they have discerned it, but because it is acceptable to them to believe! Or what errors arise because one does not go to the bottom of a thing, but forms a hasty judgment! All these reasons for deception in ordinary life might be multiplied indefinitely. What tricks are played upon sound judgment by partisan feeling, passion, and so forth. If such errors of judgment in ordinary life are disturbing and often disastrous, they are the greatest conceivable danger to the wholesomeness of the supersensible experience. No general rule can be given to the student for his guidance in the higher worlds, beyond the advice to do everything possible for his healthy power of discernment and for his sound, independent judgment.

When the observer in the higher worlds once knows what Imagination really is, he soon acquires the conviction that the pictures of the astral world are not merely pictures, but manifestations of spiritual beings. He comes to know that these imaginative pictures have reference to spirit or soul being just as do sensory colors to sensory things or beings. In particular, he will, of course, have yet much to learn. He must learn to discriminate between color formations that are opaque and those that are quite transparent and in their inner nature clear and radiant. In fact, he will perceive formations that seem to be continually producing their color-light anew from within, and that therefore are not only fully illuminated and transparent, but are forever radiating light from within. He will link the opaque formations to lower beings, the clear, luminous ones to intermediate entities; the inwardly radiant ones will be for him manifestations of higher spiritual beings.

If we would arrive at the truth about the imaginative world, we must not form too narrow a concept of spiritual sight, for in that world there are not mere light and color perceptions, comparable to the sight experiences of the

50

physical world, but also impressions of heat and cold, of taste and smell, and still other experiences of the imaginative "senses" for which the physical world offers no likeness. Impressions of heat and cold are, in the imaginative (astral) world, revelations of will and intention on the part of soul and spirit beings. Whether such a being aims at good or evil comes to light in a definite effect of heat or cold. Astral beings can also be "tasted" or "smelled."— Only what constitutes in the actual sense the physical element of tone and sound is almost wholly lacking in the real imaginative world. In this connection absolute stillness prevails there. But instead, for the progressing spiritual observer, there is offered something quite different, comparable to tone and sound, to music and speech, in the sense world. This higher element steps in when every tone and sound from the outer physical world is wholly hushed; indeed, when even the faintest inner soul echo from this sphere of the outer world is silenced. Then there occurs for the observer what may be called an understanding of the significance of the imaginative experiences. If we were to compare what is now experienced with something in the physical world we could only come near to explaining the matter by referring to something that does not exist at all in that world. Let it be supposed possible to perceive the thoughts and feelings of a human being without hearing his words with the physical ear; such a perception might be comparable to a direct comprehension of the imaginative element referred to as "hearing" in the spiritual sense. What "speaks" are the color and light impressions. In lightings-up and dimmings-down, in the color metamorphosis of images are revealed harmonies and discords that unveil the feelings, representations, and

thought life of soul and spirit beings. Just as tone becomes speech in physical man when thought is imprinted
in it, so do harmonies and discords of the spirit world grow
into manifestations that are definite thought entities. To
this end, darkness must fall upon that world if thought is
to be revealed in its immediacy. The experience here is:
The bright color-tones — red, yellow, and orange — are
seen to fade away, and it is perceived how the higher world
darkens through green to blue and violet; at the same time
a waxing of inner will energy is experienced. Full freedom
with regard to space and time is experienced; there is a
feeling of being in motion. Certain linear forms and shapes
are experienced. These are not experienced as though seen
to be drawn before one in any spatial expanse, but rather
as though in continuous movement every single curve,
every form, was followed by the ego. In fact, the ego is at
once felt as the draughtsman and the drawing material.
Every linear direction, every shift in position, is at
one and the same time an experience of this ego. The ego
stirred to motion is recognized to be bound up with the
world's creative forces. The laws of the world are no longer
something that the ego perceives outwardly, but a truly
miraculous fabric that it is helping to weave. — Occult
science designs all kinds of symbolic drawings and pictures. When these really correspond to fact and are not
mere invented figures, they are based on the observer's
experiences in higher worlds, which are to be viewed as
described above.

So is the world of Inspiration placed within the Imaginative world. When the Imaginations begin to unveil
their meanings in "silent speech" to the observer, the world
of Inspiration arises within the Imaginative world.

52

Of that world that the spiritual observer penetrates in this way, the physical is a manifestation. Whatever of the physical world is accessible to the senses and the sense-bound intellect is only the outer side. To cite a single example, the plant as observed with physical senses and physical intellect is not the whole plant being. Whoever knows only this physical plant resembles a being who might be able to perceive the finger nail of a man, but to whom the perception of man himself would be inaccessible. But the structure and being of the finger nail is understandable only when explained by the whole nature of man. Thus in truth the plant is comprehensible only when one knows what pertains to it as the whole human nature relates to the man's fingernail. But what is related to the plant cannot be found in the physical world. The plant is related to something fundamental that can only be unveiled by Imagination in the astral world, and, further, to something that will be revealed only through Inspiration in the spirit-world. — Thus the plant as a physical organism is the revelation of a being comprehensible by Imagination and Inspiration.

From the foregoing it is evident how for the observer of higher worlds there opens up a path that has its beginning in the physical world. Namely, he can start from the physical world and from its manifestations rise to the higher being sustaining them. If he starts from the animal kingdom, he can rise by this means into the imaginative world; if he takes his start from the plant world, spirit-observation will lead him through Imagination to the world of Inspiration. If this path is taken, within the imaginative and inspiration worlds will soon be found beings and facts not at all revealed in the physical world. It must not, therefore, be believed that in this way acquaintance is made only with those beings of the higher worlds that have physical manifestations. Whoever has once entered the imaginative world comes to know a multitude of beings and occurrences of which the observer of what is merely physical has not the slightest inkling.

Now, to be sure, there is another way. It does not take its start from the physical world. It makes man directly clairvoyant in the higher regions of existence. For many persons this method might have more power of attraction than the one above indicated. But for our life-conditions only the ascent from the physical world should be chosen. It requires of the observer the self-renunciation that is necessary if he is first of all to examine the physical world around him and accumulate knowledge and, especially, experience. In any case, it is the method best suited to our present-day cultural conditions. The other way presupposes the prior acquisition of soul qualities extremely hard to attain under modern life-conditions. Even though such soul qualities have again and again been stressed with full sharpness and clarity in past writings, still most people have no idea at all, or at most, an inadequate one — of the degree to which these qualities (for example, selfless-ness and devoted love) must be acquired for attainment of the higher worlds without starting from the firm ground of the physical. If anyone should be awakened in the higher worlds without having attained the requisite degree of the corresponding soul qualities, the result must be unspeakable misery. Now it must not be believed, however, that the soul qualities characterized above can be dispensed with by one making his start from the physical world and its experiences. To believe this would also be an error of serious consequences. But such a start allows for the gradual acquisition of these qualities in the measure, and above all in the form, possible in our present life conditions.

Another thing comes into consideration in this regard. If the start is made in the way indicated from the physical world, a living connection is retained with this physical world in spite of the ascent into higher worlds. A full understanding continues for all that happens in it, and the full energy to work in it. Indeed, this understanding and energy increase in a most helpful way just through the knowledge of the higher worlds. In every realm of life, even in what seems most prosaically practical, the knower of the higher worlds will work better and more usefully than the non-knower, provided he has preserved the living connection with the physical world.

But whoever is awakened in the higher spheres of existence without starting from the physical world is only too readily estranged from life; he becomes a hermit, confronting his contemporaries without understanding or sympathy. Indeed, it even happens that people of incomplete development in this respect — not, of course, those with perfect development — look down with a certain disdain upon the experiences of the physical world and feel themselves superior, and so forth. Instead of their sympathy toward the world being heightened, such people become hardened, self-seeking natures in the spiritual sense. The temptation to all this is truly not slight, and those striving for the ascent into the higher worlds may well pay attention to it.

From Inspiration the spiritual observer may rise to Intuition. In the manner of expression of occult science this word denotes in many respects the exact opposite of that for which it is often used in ordinary life. In the ordinary sense intuition is spoken of when one has in view a notion dimly felt to be true, which still lacks clear, conceptual definition. A preliminary step toward knowledge, rather than knowledge itself, is seen therein. An idea of this nature may — according to that definition — illuminate a great truth like a flash of lightning, but it can first have value as knowledge when founded on conceptual judgment. Sometimes also intuition designates something "felt" as truth, of which one is fully convinced, but which one will not weigh down with intellectual judgment. People who become acquainted with spiritual-scientific knowledge, often say: That was always clear to me "intuitively." All this must be put entirely aside if the term Intuition is to be kept in view in its true significance meant here. In this application Intuition is not a mode of cognition which with regard to clarity lags behind intellectual knowledge, but one that far surpasses it.

In Inspiration the experiences of the higher worlds speak their meaning. The observer lives in the qualities and actions of the beings of these higher worlds. If, as described above, he follows with his ego a lineal direction or the shape of a figure, he knows that he is not within the being itself, but within its qualities and functions. Already in imaginative cognition he has, indeed, experienced the feeling of being not outside, but inside the color-images; but he knows no less clearly that these color-images are not in themselves independent beings, but the qualities of such beings. In Inspiration, he is conscious of his becoming one with the deeds of such beings, with the manifestations of their will; in Intuition, for the first time, he merges

56

his own self into that of self-contained beings. This can happen in the right way only if the mergence takes place, not by the effacement, but by the complete maintenance of his own being. Any "losing of oneself" in another being is bad. Therefore only an ego fortified to a high degree within itself can without damage plunge into another being. — Something has been grasped intuitively only if the feeling has arisen with regard to it that in it there is expressing itself a being of the self-same nature and inner content as one's own ego. Whoever examines a stone with his outer senses and seeks to understand its peculiarities with his intellect and by the usual scientific resources comes to know only the outer aspect of the stone. As spiritual observer he proceeds to imaginative and inspired knowledge. By dwelling within Inspiration he can come to an additional feeling. This may be characterized in the following way by a comparison. Suppose one sees a man on the street. To begin with, he makes a fleeting impression upon the observer. Later one becomes better acquainted with him; then comes the moment when one becomes such a friend that soul opens itself to soul. The experience goes through when the veils of the soul fall thus away and one ego confronts the other, is comparable to that when, to the spiritual observer the stone appears solely as an outer manifestation, and he advances to something related to the stone as the fingernail to the human body, and which lives itself out as an ego like one's own ego.

That kind of knowledge that leads into the "innermost nature" of beings is first attained for man in Intuition. In the discussion of Inspiration, mention has been made of the transformation the spiritual observer's inner soul constitution must undergo if he wishes to arrive at this mode of cognition. In this connection it has been stated that, for instance, an incorrect conclusion must extend its effects not only to the intellect, but to the sensing nature, that it must cause grief, pain, and the observer must systematically cultivate such inner experience. Of course, as long as this pain springs from the sympathies and antipathies of the ego, and from partisan attitudes, the preparation for Inspiration cannot be considered adequate. Such involvement of the soul is far removed from the inner sympathy that the ego must feel for the pure truth — as truth — if it would arrive at the proclaimed goal. If cannot be too strongly emphasized that all forms of interest that prevail in ordinary life as pleasure and pain in relation to truth and error, must first be silenced, and then a totally different kind of interest, wholly without self-seeking, must enter in if anything is to be done for cognition through Inspiration. This one quality of the inner soul life is, however, but one means of preparation for Inspiration. There is an unlimited number of others that must be added to it, and the more the spiritual observer refines himself with regard to what has already served him for Inspiration, the better equipped he will be to approach Intuition.

RECOVERING THE SOURCES OF MEANING:
THE PATH OF ANTHROPOSOPHY

Anthroposophy, which means "the wisdom of the human being," is not just an abstract philosophy but a living spiritual path that reconnects human beings to the universe and to the sources of what it means to be human. Rudolf Steiner, who renewed this path of meaning in our time, saw four of his books as fundamental to the recovery of human dignity. Despite the many other books he wrote and the more than 6,000 lectures he gave, Steiner returned again and again to these four basic books.

The Basic Books

The Philosophy of Spiritual Activity

This fundamental work of philosophy demonstrates the fact of freedom — the ability to think and act independently — as a possibility for modern consciousness. Read properly, the book leads the reader to experience the living thinking by which all human activity may be renewed.

Knowledge of Higher Worlds and its Attainment

This is the fundamental guide to the anthroposophical path of knowledge. In human consciousness faculties sleep that, if awoken, lead to life-giving wisdom. With great clarity and warmth Steiner details the exercises and moral qualities to be cultivated on the path to conscious experience of supersensible realities.

Theosophy

This work, subtitled "An Introduction to the Supersensible Knowledge of the World and Human Destiny," begins by describing the threefold nature of the human being: the body or sense-world, the soul or inner world, the spirit or universal world of cosmic archetypes. A profound discussion of reincarnation and karma follows, concluding with a description of the soul's journey through the supersensible regions after death. The book closes with an outline of the path to higher knowledge.

An Outline of Occult Science

This masterwork of esotericism places humanity at the heart of the vast, invisible processes of cosmic evolution. Descriptions of the different members of the human being, in themselves and in relation to sleep and death, are followed by a profound investigation of cosmic evolution and the beings that direct it. The book concludes with a detailed, practical guide to the methods by which such "initiation" knowledge may be attained.

Related titles

Christianity as Mystical Fact

Christianity arose out of what was prepared in the pre-Christian Mysteries. However, Christianity was not merely a further development of what existed in these Mysteries but something unique and independent. Against this background, the book includes discussions of the Gospels, the raising of Lazarus, the Apocalypse, and the historical background of Jesus.

The Christmas Conference 1923/24

The Laying of the Foundation Stone in the hearts of the assembled members forms the center of this elegant and beautiful book that documents the founding of the General Anthroposophical Society. The Foundation Stone Mantra is reproduced in the form that Rudolf Steiner gave it on each day of the Conference, together with his comments on the mantra's various rhythms.

Four Mystery Dramas

These four plays, depicting the experiences of a group of people and their relationships as they go on a path of spiritual development, contain the essence of anthroposophy.

The Calendar of the Soul

Steiner's fifty-two meditative verses help one to participate actively in the life of the year as it unfolds week by week.

The Course of My Life

This is Steiner's remarkable autobiography in which he traces his life through his forty-sixth year. Rather than focussing on outer events, he describes the path of his soul development and the struggles he went through to develop his world view.

Other authors

Water: The Element of Life
by Theodor and Wolfram Schwenk

This outstanding collection of essays by the author of *Sensitive Chaos* and his son ranges over a wide range of topics from the cosmic significance of water to its behavior and nutritive value. Above all, the authors convincingly depict the earth as a living organism, with water as its sense organ, perceiving cosmic life-giving forces and allowing them to enter our earthly realm. As the authors explain, it is the living movement of water that makes life on earth possible. Their solutions for the current water and ecological crises go beyond piecemeal measures to a comprehensive and radical "water consciousness."

Encountering the Self: Transformation and Destiny in the Ninth Year
by Hermann Koepke

The author, a Waldorf teacher of many years experience, provides a lucid explanation of the events occurring in the life of a child between the ninth and the tenth year. This is the time when the child's I incarnates more deeply. As a result, children at this age experience themselves for the first time as separate individuals, an experience often accompanied by a first encounter with death, a first inkling that life is fragile and does not go on forever.

For prices and a catalogue of titles published and distributed
by Anthroposophic Press, please write to:

Anthroposophic Press
RR4, Box 94 A-1,
Hudson, New York 12534
Telephone: 518-851-2054